ELK GROVE VILLAGE PUBLIC LIBRARY
1001 WELLINGTON AVE
ELK GROVE VILLAGE, IL 60007
(847) 439-0447

THE STORY OF THE

FIESTA
BOWL

by Barry Wilner

SportsZone

An Imprint of Abdo Publishing | abdopublishing.com

abdopublishing.com

Published by Abdo Publishing, a division of ABDO, PO Box 398166, Minneapolis, Minnesota 55439. Copyright © 2016 by Abdo Consulting Group, Inc. International copyrights reserved in all countries. No part of this book may be reproduced in any form without written permission from the publisher. SportsZone™ is a trademark and logo of Abdo Publishing.

Printed in the United States of America, North Mankato, Minnesota
052015
092015

Cover Photo: Charles Krupa/AP Images, cover
Interior Photos: Charles Krupa/AP Images, 1, 28; AP Images, 4, 6; Lennox McLendon/AP Images, 7; Eric Risberg/AP Images, 8; Rob Schumacher/AP Images, 10, 13; Aaron J. Latham/AP Images, 14; Dave Martin/AP Images, 16, 19; Mark Humphrey/AP Images, 20; Lenny Ignelzi/AP Images, 22; Mark J. Terrill/AP Images, 26; Ted S. Warren/File/AP Images, 25; Ted S. Warren/AP Images, 31, 32; Matt York/AP Images, 36, 39; Ross D. Franklin/AP Images, 40; David Seibert/AP Images, 42; Bob Galbraith/AP Images, 43

Editor: Patrick Donnelly
Series Designer: Nikki Farinella

Library of Congress Control Number: 2015931694

Cataloging-in-Publication Data
Wilner, Barry.
 The story of the Fiesta Bowl / Barry Wilner.
   p. cm. -- (Bowl games of college football)
Includes bibliographical references and index.
ISBN 978-1-62403-888-4
1. Fiesta Bowl (Football game)--History--Juvenile literature. 2. Football--United States--Juvenile literature. 3. College sports--Juvenile literature. I. Title.
796.332--dc23
                                                        2015931694

TABLE OF CONTENTS

Florida State safety David Snell, 20, returns a kick against Arizona State in the first Fiesta Bowl on December 27, 1971.

FIESTA BOWL HISTORY:
TAKING ROOT IN THE DESERT

The college football world looked a lot different in the 1960s. At the time, the Rose, Orange, Sugar, and Cotton Bowl games dominated the scene. There were a few other bowls, but college football fans paid the most attention to those four. The games were usually played on New Year's Day. When they were all wrapped up, the national champion was crowned.

Some folks in Phoenix, Arizona, figured their climate was warm enough to stage a bowl game, too. In 1968, Arizona State University President G. Homer Durham came up with the idea of creating a bowl game for the Phoenix area. There was no name for it yet, but there was lots of interest. College football was plenty popular in the state. Two local schools—the University

Oklahoma State quarterback Scott Burk, *center*, fights off a Brigham Young tackler in the 1974 Fiesta Bowl. Oklahoma State won 16–6.

of Arizona in Tucson and Arizona State University (ASU) in Tempe—were members of the Western Athletic Conference (WAC).

Back then, even though ASU had a strong team, the WAC was viewed as a weak league. In 1969, the Sun Devils were not invited to a bowl game despite posting an 8-2 record. That upset Arizonans, who believed it was time for a postseason college game in the Southwest.

The local newspaper, the *Arizona Republic*, backed the idea. So did many Phoenix-area businesses. Soon, a

Penn State coach Joe Paterno, *left*, and Arizona State coach Frank Kush pose for pictures before the 1977 Fiesta Bowl.

plan was presented to the National Collegiate Athletic Association (NCAA), which is in charge of college sports.

In 1970, ASU went 10–0 but only was invited to the second-level Peach Bowl. And the NCAA shot down the Arizona bowl idea. But the boosters in Phoenix did not give up. They improved their plan, and the next year, the NCAA approved the new bowl.

The next step was to name the annual bowl game. A public contest was held, and *Fiesta*, which means "party" or "festival" in Spanish, was the winner.

Michigan coach Bo Schembechler, *center*, is carried off the field by his players after the Wolverines beat Nebraska 27–23 in the Fiesta Bowl on January 1, 1986.

So Arizona had a new bowl game, which would be played at Sun Devil Stadium on the ASU campus. And it had a name. Next it needed two teams to play in it—and not just for the first year, but every year as the Fiesta Bowl tried to become better known.

The organizers wanted their game to be just as big as the Rose, Orange, Sugar, and Cotton Bowls. They wanted to have the very best teams in college football—Alabama, Oklahoma, Notre Dame, Penn State—come to Tempe.

But first the bowl would have to prove itself worthy. The hometown Sun Devils were chosen to play in the first Fiesta Bowl. And the host team from the western United States would need to show it could play with and beat top teams from other parts of the country.

ASU was the home team before 51,000 fans on December 27, 1971, for the first Fiesta Bowl. That day the Sun Devils beat Florida State 45–38 behind Danny White, a future Dallas Cowboys quarterback.

The game increased in importance throughout the 1970s. In 1978, the University of Arizona and ASU joined the Pacific-10 Conference. By 1980, football fans considered the Fiesta Bowl a big-time game. Penn State beat Ohio State 31–19 that year in the first game that did not feature a team from the WAC or Pacific-10. The following season, the Fiesta Bowl moved to New Year's Day, joining the other major bowls. That year Penn State beat Southern California and future Hall of Fame running back Marcus Allen 26–10.

The little bowl game that had begun only a decade earlier now was one of the big boys.

HOMETOWN HEROES

The first three Fiesta Bowls were home games for ASU. After the Sun Devils beat Florida State in the first one, they downed Missouri and Pittsburgh the next two years. In fact, they won four of the first five Fiesta Bowls, also beating Nebraska in 1975.

Penn State linebacker Shane Conlan, *left*, catches Miami running back Warren Williams by the facemask in the second quarter of the 1987 Fiesta Bowl.

2

1987: FIESTA COMBAT

Penn State vs. Miami

The controversy started the minute the Miami Hurricanes walked off the airplane at the Phoenix airport. When the Penn State players arrived for the Fiesta Bowl, they were wearing suits. The Hurricanes were decked out in camouflage, as if ready for battle.

That set the tone for a wild week in Arizona as top-ranked Miami and number-two Penn State got ready to decide the national championship.

"People need to understand, we didn't have a dress code," said Hurricanes defensive end Daniel Stubbs.

Miami coach Jimmy Johnson and athletic director Sam Jankovich had flown to Phoenix before the team. That left it up to the players to decide what to wear on the plane ride from Florida. At a cookout for the teams later in the week, the Nittany Lions again wore suits, whereas the Hurricanes donned black sweatsuits.

After Penn State players performed a skit making fun of some of the Hurricanes, the Miami players skipped their chance to return the favor. Instead, they rose as a team and walked out.

"We said, 'We're not here to do a show,'" Stubbs recalled.

On the football field, both were used to putting on a defensive show. In 11 games, Penn State had given up only 123 points and Miami had allowed 136.

Each team had All-America players on both sides of the ball. Miami quarterback Vinny Testaverde had won the Heisman Trophy that year as college football's best player. Meanwhile, safety Bennie Blades and defensive tackle Jerome Brown led the defense. Penn State running back D. J. Dozier controlled the ground game for the Nittany Lions, and Shane Conlan was the latest outstanding linebacker at a school known for producing them regularly. Both had successful coaches in Johnson and the legendary Joe Paterno.

The first quarter was scoreless, hardly a surprise given how the teams played defense. Penn State showed early on that Miami was not the only team that could

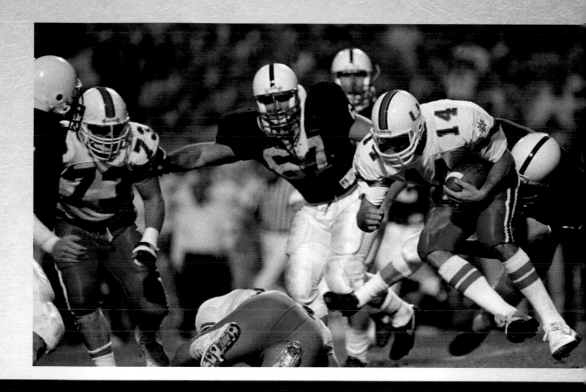

be intimidating. Nittany Lions defenders hit Miami receivers Michael Irvin and Brian Blades so hard that it looked as if neither player would return to the game. They both did, but neither played well after taking those shots.

"Our little, slow guys back there just rocked 'em, and soon they didn't want to catch the ball," Conlan said. "Later on, we were helping their receivers up after we hit them and patting them on their butts. Receivers hate that."

The Fiesta Bowl trophy

Miami finally opened the scoring on a 1-yard run by Melvin Bratton in the second quarter. But Penn State answered with a 74-yard drive, by far its best work so far in the game. Quarterback John Shaffer scored on a 4-yard run and it was 7–7 at halftime.

After a scoreless third quarter, Miami's Mark Seelig made a 38-yard field goal early in the fourth. That put the Hurricanes on top 10–7. Penn State failed to move the ball on its next series and punted. The Nittany Lions' hopes were fading.

Then Conlan stepped up. He picked off Testaverde's pass—his second interception of the game and Penn

State's fourth pick against the Heisman Trophy winner. Conlan returned it 38 yards to the Miami 5-yard line. Two plays later, Dozier scored for a 14–10 lead.

But with Miami's offensive weapons, the game was far from over. Testaverde hit Brian Blades for 31 yards on a fourth-down play to keep the drive alive. After six straight completions, Miami had driven inside the Penn State 10-yard line with less than a minute remaining. But the Nittany Lions defense held tough for three downs. The national title would come down to one play.

Once more, Penn State's defense would save the day. Linebacker Pete Giftopoulos stepped in front of receiver Brett Perriman and intercepted Testaverde's pass. Giftopoulos fell to his knees as the other Nittany Lions celebrated.

"It came down to one play," Paterno said. "If we make it, we win the national championship. If they make it, they win the national championship."

Penn State made the play and won a Fiesta Bowl for the ages.

TROPHY TALK

Since 2003 the winner of the game has received the Fiesta Bowl Trophy. It stands 46 inches (117 cm) high and weighs approximately 200 pounds (90 kg). The base and platform are carved from marble, and the figures on the trophy are made of sterling silver. On top is a football made of gold with the Fiesta Bowl logo on it and diamonds for football stripes.

Tennessee quarterback Tee Martin avoids two Florida State defenders as he runs for a first down in the 1999 Fiesta Bowl.

3

1999:
WHO NEEDS PEYTON?
Tennessee vs. Florida State

Peyton Manning was the greatest quarterback ever to play at Tennessee. He set all kinds of records from 1994 to 1997 as a Tennessee Volunteer, or "Vol." But the first overall pick in the 1998 National Football League (NFL) Draft never won a national championship at Tennessee

When Tee Martin took over as Tennessee's quarterback in 1998, expectations were low. Sure, the Vols would be good, but champions? Probably not.

Then Tennessee got on a roll. It won all 11 regular-season games, including a 20–17 win over Florida, a team Manning never beat. The Vols were the top-ranked team in the nation when they beat Mississippi State to clinch the Southeastern Conference (SEC). That sent them off to Tempe, where they would play number-two Florida State in the first Bowl Championship Series (BCS) final. The BCS was a system that matched up the top teams in the biggest four bowl games. It ensured that the first- and second-ranked teams met for the championship.

One side of Sun Devil Stadium was a sea of orange as Tennessee fans sported their team's colors. The other side was filled with the garnet and gold of Florida State, champions of the Atlantic Coast Conference.

Volunteers fans sang the traditional Tennessee song "Rocky Top" as loudly as they could. Florida State fans did their "tomahawk chop" as strongly as they could.

The Seminoles had one of the fastest receivers and kick returners in football, Peter Warrick. He would need to be a star against Tennessee if the Seminoles were to have a chance.

The first big play came from Martin and his top receiver, Peerless Price. The word *peerless* means "without equal," and Price would be just that in this Fiesta Bowl. Martin hooked up with Price on a 76-yard pass. Four plays later, Shawn Bryson caught a 4-yard pass from Martin to make it 7-0.

Florida State needed to answer quickly. Instead, Tennessee's Dwayne Goodrich intercepted

Tennessee's Dwayne Goodrich, *left*, rips the ball away from Florida State wide receiver Peter Warrick. Goodrich returned the interception for a touchdown that put the Vols on top 14–0.

The scoreboard says it all—Tennessee had won the Fiesta Bowl and the national championship.

Marcus Outzen's pass and returned it 54 yards to the end zone just 25 seconds after Bryson's touchdown. Tennessee led 14–0 and "Rocky Top" shook the building.

The Seminoles were not ready to give up. They came right back in the second quarter with William McCray's 1-yard run and a field goal by Sebastian Janikowski. Florida State missed its extra point after McCray's touchdown, so at halftime Tennessee led 14–9.

Neither team scored in the third quarter. The national title would be decided in the final 15 minutes of the season. The heroes would be Martin and Price.

Even though Warrick had come into the game with the high-flying reputation, Tennessee's Price was the game's brightest star. He blew by the Seminoles' defense on a 79-yard touchdown pass from Martin. At the time it was the longest pass play in Fiesta Bowl history. Another missed extra point kept the lead at 20-9, but it held up. Tennessee's Jeff Hall added a field goal, and even though Outzen ran for a touchdown late in the game, it was not enough for Florida State.

Rock on, Rocky Top: Tennessee 23, Florida State 16. Tennessee had its first national championship since 1951. The difference makers were Martin and Price. Martin threw for 278 yards, 199 of them to Price. Tennessee's title was not expected so soon after Manning headed to the NFL. That made it even sweeter for the Vols.

BCS BOWLERS

From 1998 to 2013, the Fiesta Bowl was part of the BCS. It hosted the BCS championship game two times. Starting in 2007, a separate national championship game was held at a BCS bowl site, but one week after the bowl. So in 2007 and in 2011, University of Phoenix Stadium hosted a Fiesta Bowl and the national title game.

Miami tight end Kellen Winslow Jr., *right*, hauls in a touchdown pass over Ohio State's Will Allen in the 2003 Fiesta Bowl.

4

2003: CHAMPION BUCKEYES
Ohio State vs. Miami

The longest game in Fiesta Bowl history was a matchup for the national title between top-ranked Miami and number-two Ohio State. It was one of the wildest, too.

Miami had become the toast of college football. The defending national champions had won 34 straight games. Ohio State, one of the game's most famous programs, had not won the national crown in 34 years.

The Hurricanes (12-0) had scored 503 points during the season and had scored at least 26 points in every game. The Buckeyes (13-0) had won the Big Ten Conference, but six of their wins came by seven points or fewer. Ohio State was not afraid of Miami, though.

"We're very comfortable, and we're going to come out and surprise some people," linebacker Matt Wilhelm said.

An Ohio State victory would be a big surprise to Miami's players and its fans. The Hurricanes had four All-Americans: running back Willis McGahee, quarterback Ken Dorsey, center Brett Romberg, and defensive tackle Jerome McDougle. They knew how to win the biggest of games.

So when the game started and Dorsey hit Roscoe Parrish for a 25-yard touchdown, that was to be expected. When Ohio State came right back with two touchdowns on short runs and led 14–7 at halftime, well, that was more of a surprise.

The Buckeyes' defense had stopped Miami's strong offense for most of the half, and Ohio State even added a field goal in the third quarter for a 17–7 lead. Then the Hurricanes got down to business, scoring 10 straight points to tie the game. Todd Sievers kicked a 40-yard field goal as time expired to force the first Fiesta Bowl overtime.

Then things *really* got interesting.

In college football overtime, each team gets a chance to score from the other team's 25-yard line. The Hurricanes got the ball first in overtime and scored on a

Ohio State tailback Maurice Clarett dives into the end zone for a 5-yard touchdown, putting the Buckeyes ahead in the second overtime of the 2003 Fiesta Bowl.

7-yard touchdown catch by tight end Kellen Winslow Jr. If they could stop Ohio State from getting into the end zone, they would carry home the Fiesta Bowl trophy and another national championship.

And the Hurricanes thought they did just that. They stopped Ohio State cold on three plays, leaving the Buckeyes with a do-or-die fourth-down play. But Ohio State quarterback Craig Krenzel connected with receiver Michael Jenkins for 17 yards and a first down.

Ohio State quarterback Craig Krenzel, *center*, celebrates his game-saving touchdown in overtime against Miami.

So Miami held on the next three plays, forcing another fourth down with the title on the line. This time Krenzel passed to Chris Gamble and the ball fell to the ground. Miami players began celebrating, thinking they had won. But a few seconds after the ball hit the ground—very late for a penalty to be called—the officials threw a flag for pass interference.

That gave Ohio State a first down at the 2-yard line. Krenzel then scored on a touchdown run on third down, and the extra point made it 24–24. On to the second overtime.

The Hurricanes were still in shock from what happened at the end of the first overtime. Ohio State got the ball first in the second overtime. The Buckeyes' top running back, Maurice Clarett, scored from 5 yards out. Now Miami would have to score to keep their title hopes alive.

The Hurricanes came close, getting down to the 1-yard line. But on fourth down, the Buckeyes' Cie Grant blitzed and forced Dorsey to heave a pass into the air. Wilhelm knocked it to the ground. Ohio State had a 31–24 win in double overtime.

The Hurricanes could not believe how close they had come to winning, only to fall excruciatingly short.

"It feels unreal," Miami fullback Quadtrine Hill said. "After the game was over, it felt like we had one play left. It can't be over. It's something I never want to feel again."

CONFERENCE CONNECTIONS

The WAC champion received an automatic bid to the Fiesta Bowl from 1971 to 1978. But that relationship ended when ASU and the University of Arizona jumped to the Pacific-10 Conference. For the next 20 years, the Fiesta Bowl organizers were free to offer bids to the best schools they could find. Beginning in 1999, the champion of the Big 12 Conference was granted an automatic bid to the Fiesta Bowl if they were not playing for the national championship.

Oklahoma quarterback Paul Thompson, *center*, is brought down by a host of Boise State defenders during the 2007 Fiesta Bowl.

5

2007: BOISE STATE'S SHOCKER

Boise State vs. Oklahoma

Boise State was new to all this bowl stuff. Sure, over the years it had dominated smaller conferences—the Big Sky, Big West, and WAC. But those conferences are not considered to be big-league in stature. Boise State had gone to bowl games since 1999, but mostly the lower-level ones. In fact, the Broncos did not leave Boise for their first three postseason trips. The Idaho school hosted and won the Humanitarian Bowl in 1999, 2000, and 2002.

The Broncos also made trips to other smaller games, too. But now, at last, they had hit the big time. The 12–0 Broncos finally had been recognized as good enough to play a top team in a bowl game. The opponent was Oklahoma out of the Big 12 Conference.

The Sooners carried an 11-2 record into the first Fiesta Bowl at the new University of Phoenix Stadium. This was Boise State's seventh bowl game ever; it was the fortieth for Oklahoma, which had won seven national championships.

Despite their perfect record, the Broncos had no shot at a national title. The national polls ranked them ninth in the country because they played a weaker schedule. But the players believed they were ready for the challenge.

"We've got a bunch of really confident guys walking around with huge chips on their shoulders," Boise State quarterback Jared Zabransky said, "ready to prove a point that we deserve to be here."

From the opening kickoff, Boise State showed it could play with Oklahoma. The Broncos took a 14-0 lead on a long touchdown pass by Zabransky and a short touchdown run by tailback Ian Johnson. That was just the beginning of a big night for both players.

Oklahoma was not the type of team to get nervous when it fell behind. The Sooners scored the next 10 points as they figured out how to slow down the smaller but very quick Broncos.

But Boise State had learned the same lessons about staying calm and sticking to its game plan.

Boise State quarterback Jared Zabransky, *center*, hands the ball off behind his back to tailback Ian Johnson. The trick play in overtime gave the Broncos the victory over Oklahoma.

The Broncos came right back with another touchdown pass by Zabransky and an interception return by Marty Tadman for a score. Boise State led 28–10. Was it time for Oklahoma to get anxious?

Not really. The Sooners had the nation's best running back, Adrian Peterson, who would go on to star in the NFL. Peterson began making some key runs, including an 8-yard scamper for a touchdown. With time ticking away, Oklahoma got a 5-yard touchdown pass from Paul Thompson to Quentin Chaney. Then Thompson hit Juaquin Iglesias for a two-point conversion to tie the game at 28.

Boise State's strong offense got the ball back with 1:26 left. But Zabransky threw his only interception of the night, and Marcus Walker ran it 33 yards into the end zone. For the first time, the Sooners led 35–28.

"It would have been easy to give up on us with a minute left, but we had a lot of magic left," Zabransky said.

Indeed they did. Zabransky led the Broncos to midfield, but then Oklahoma held firm. On fourth-and-18, what could the Broncos possibly come up with to stay alive? They dialed up one of the oldest trick plays in the book. And it worked to perfection.

Zabransky passed to Drisan James at Oklahoma's 35. James caught it, then pitched the ball to teammate Jerard Rabb. The Sooners got suckered by the "hook and lateral" play. Not only did Rabb have some open field, he raced all the way into the end zone with seven seconds left.

Boise fans went crazy in the stands. Oklahoma fans couldn't believe their eyes. The Broncos made the extra-point kick and the game was headed to overtime.

Yet even in the overtime, fans wondered if the Broncos had any gas left in their tanks. When Peterson broke free on a 25-yard touchdown run on the first play of the extra period, Oklahoma seemed in control.

Except the Broncos had not run out of miracles. Sure, they did not have anyone as skilled as Peterson. But they were gutsy and creative. After five plays, they were at the Sooners 5-yard line. Again, it was fourth down. Again, the Broncos drew up a play that would be remembered forever.

Coach Chris Petersen ordered a pass, but not by quarterback Zabransky. Wide receiver Vinny Perretta took a direct snap on what looked like a sweeping run. But Perretta stopped and threw to Derek Schouman in the end zone for a touchdown.

The Broncos still weren't finished. They had one more trick up their sleeves. Petersen decided he wanted to end the game right then and there. "They are so physical up front—we had to try something a little different," he said. So the Broncos went for a two-point conversion rather than force a second overtime.

Petersen called for the "Statue of Liberty" play. It had pretty much disappeared from college football years before the Fiesta Bowl was born. But Boise gave it a shot. Zabransky dropped back as if to pass and faked a throw to the right. Then Johnson came behind the quarterback running the other way, and Zabransky handed him the ball behind his back.

Oklahoma was completely fooled. Johnson surged into the end zone for the winning two points, threw the ball into the stands, and was mobbed by fans. Then, live on national TV, he found his cheerleader girlfriend and asked her to marry him. (She said yes.) Football fans everywhere now knew all about Boise State.

"We went 13-0 and beat everyone on our schedule," said Zabransky, the game's offensive Most Valuable Player (MVP). "We deserve a chance at the national title."

UNBEATEN BUT UNNOTICED

Boise State was the only unbeaten team in the NCAA's top division during the 2006 season. Yet the Broncos were ranked number 5 at the end of the season because they did not play a tough schedule. Florida out of the mighty SEC went 12–1 and beat Ohio State for the title.

Central Florida quarterback Blake Bortles tries to escape a tackle against Baylor in the 2014 Fiesta Bowl.

6

2014:
LIGHTING UP
THE SCOREBOARD

Baylor vs. Central Florida

P oints often come easily in the Fiesta Bowl. Scores of past games have included 41–38, 48–28, 43 42, and even a 62-24 win for Nebraska over Florida in 1996. In 2014, Central Florida and Baylor took it to another level.

The Baylor Bears, from the Big 12 Conference, were expected to win easily. Central Florida (UCF), coming out of the new American Athletic Conference (AAC), was playing in its first BCS bowl. Baylor had scored 67 and 49 points in its past two bowls, both wins.

Was the Fiesta Bowl looking at a mismatch even though both teams had 11–1 records? Perhaps not.

"Our motivation is we're in a BCS bowl game and we're trying to put [Central Florida] on the map," linebacker Terrance Plummer said. "This is our prime-time game. We want everyone to know about us, so as a team we're not worried about what others have to say about us."

The biggest problem for the Knights was that, despite their strong record, they had not played anyone nearly as good as Baylor. The Bears had scored at least 30 points in all of their wins. Their only loss came against another Big 12 power, Oklahoma State. The Bears averaged 624.5 yards per game, the second-best total in major college history. And they led the nation in scoring with 53.3 points a game.

Central Florida won all eight of its AAC games, but six of those victories were by seven points or fewer. So the Knights had an uphill battle ahead of them. But they were not intimidated. They surged up that mountain. Or rather, they "stormed" up it.

Running back Storm Johnson scored two quick touchdowns. Before the Bears knew what hit them, Central Florida led 14–0. Knights fans who made the long trip from Orlando, Florida, to Arizona must have felt as if they were on a thrilling Disney World ride.

No team could hold down Baylor for too long, though. The Knights got sloppy, turning over the ball on three straight plays. Soon the Bears scored two

Baylor quarterback Bryce Petty, *front*, runs for a touchdown against Central Florida in the 2014 Fiesta Bowl.

touchdowns and the race was on. As the scoring went back and forth—Baylor quarterback Bryce Petty's fourth touchdown of the game tied it 28–28 in the third quarter—it became clear neither team could stop the other.

Then Central Florida's star quarterback, Blake Bortles, took over. He passed for a touchdown and then ran for one. Baylor could not catch up.

Central Florida defensive back Jordan Ozerities, *left*, tries to chase down Baylor running back Lache Seastrunk in the 2014 Fiesta Bowl.

Final score: underdog Central Florida 52, Baylor 42. It was the biggest win in school history.

"UCF played an outstanding game," Baylor coach Art Briles said. "They came out hot and fast early and we never really recovered."

Bortles, Johnson, and Rannell Hall were the heroes for the Knights. The strong-armed Bortles threw for 301 yards and three touchdowns. He also ran for 93 yards and another score. Such a great showing impressed not only Briles and Baylor, but the dozens of pro scouts at the Fiesta Bowl. Few fans had even heard of Bortles before the game. But four months later the Jacksonville Jaguars chose Bortles with the third overall pick in the NFL Draft.

Johnson, who also wound up with the NFL's Jaguars, ran for 124 yards and three scores. Wide receiver Hall, who stayed at Central Florida for the 2014 season, had four catches for 113 yards and two touchdowns against Baylor.

When the Knights were presented with the Fiesta Bowl trophy, the players held it high. Their fans chanted "UCF! UCF!" in an otherwise empty stadium. Bortles knew best what the victory meant.

"There's not many outside of us who believe we had a chance, but we did, and I think we showed what UCF football is all about," he said.

BIGGEST BLOWOUT

In the biggest mismatch in Fiesta Bowl history, Nebraska thumped Florida 62–24 in 1996. The Cornhuskers and Gators were ranked first and second in the nation, respectively. Both were undefeated. Nebraska was voted national champion after rushing for a bowl-record 524 yards. Tommie Frazier ran for 199 yards, the most by any quarterback in a bowl game. The Huskers defense dominated too, getting seven sacks and a safety and returning an interception for a touchdown.

TIMELINE

1968

Arizona State University (ASU) President G. Homer Durham has an idea to bring a bowl game to the Phoenix area.

1971

The NCAA approves the bid from a Phoenix group for a bowl game for December.

1971

On December 27, ASU beats Florida State 45–38 in the first Fiesta Bowl, played at Sun Devil Stadium on the ASU campus.

1972

ASU gains 718 yards, at the time a record for any bowl game, as it beats Missouri 49–35.

1974

The first Fiesta Bowl shown on network TV sees Oklahoma State beat Brigham Young 16–6 on CBS.

1978

The University of California, Los Angeles (UCLA) and Arkansas play the only tie in Fiesta Bowl history, 10–10.

1982

The Fiesta Bowl moves to New Year's Day, and Penn State beats Southern California 26–10.

1983

Oklahoma's Marcus Dupree runs all over ASU, gaining 239 yards. But he does not get into the end zone and the Sun Devils beat the Sooners 32–21.

1987

For the first time in a Fiesta Bowl, the nation's two top-ranked teams face off. Number-two Penn State beats number-one Miami 14–10. It was the most-watched bowl game on TV through 2014.

1996

Nebraska rocks Florida 62–24 to clinch the national title and set a Fiesta Bowl scoring record.

1997

The Fiesta Bowl becomes part of the new BCS, joining the Sugar, Orange, and Rose Bowls.

1999

Tennessee defeats Florida State 23–16 in the first BCS national title game played in the Fiesta Bowl.

2003

Ohio State outlasts Miami 31–24 in double overtime for the second BCS national title decided in the Fiesta Bowl.

2005

Utah finishes a perfect season by beating Pittsburgh 35–7.

2007

The first Fiesta Bowl not played in Sun Devil Stadium is held in the new retractable-roof stadium in Glendale, Arizona. It is the first college football game at University of Phoenix Stadium. Boise State beats Oklahoma 43–42 in overtime in perhaps the most thrilling Fiesta Bowl game ever.

2010

For the first time in college football, two non-BCS teams make it to BCS bowls. Boise State of the Western Athletic Conference beats Texas Christian of the Mountain West Conference 17–10, finishing the season 13–0 under head coach Chris Petersen.

2014

The highest-scoring game in Fiesta Bowl history sees Central Florida upset Baylor 52–42. The teams combine for 1,106 yards on offense.

BOWL RECORDS

Most passing yards
451, Browning Nagle, Louisville vs. Alabama, 1991

Most pass attempts
59, Colt McCoy, Texas vs. Ohio State, 2009

Most completions
41, Colt McCoy, Texas, vs. Ohio State, 2009

Most touchdown passes
5, Peter Tom Willis, Florida State vs. Nebraska, 1990

Most rushing yards
239, Marcus Dupree, Oklahoma vs. ASU, 1983

Most touchdowns rushing
4, Woody Green, ASU vs. Missouri, 1972

Longest run from scrimmage
84 yards, Chafie Fields, Penn State vs. Texas, 1997

Most receptions
15, Paris Warren, Utah vs. Pittsburgh, 2005

Most receiving yards
206, Darnell McDonald, Kansas State vs. Syracuse, 1998

Longest reception
85 yards, Santonio Holmes, Ohio State vs. Notre Dame, 2006

Most tackles
18, Ted Johnson, Colorado vs. Notre Dame, 1995; Matt Millen, Penn State vs. ASU, 1977; Lynn Evans, Missouri vs. ASU, 1972

Most sacks
3, Mike Kudla, Ohio State vs. Notre Dame, 2006; Tommy Hackenbruck, Utah vs. Pittsburgh, 2005; Shannon Clavelle, Colorado vs. Notre Dame, 1995

Most interceptions
3, Steve Smith, Oregon vs. Colorado, 2002

Most points scored
62, Nebraska 62, Florida 24, 1996

*through the December 2014 Fiesta Bowl

QUOTES AND ANECDOTES

When the Miami Hurricanes players came off the airplane in Phoenix for the 1987 game, most of them were wearing military camouflage outfits. One player who was not was receiver Michael Irvin, who would go on to become a Pro Football Hall of Famer. Where was his army uniform?

"We couldn't find a place that had my size," Irvin said.

Miami center Brett Romberg was asked before the 2003 game about being from Canada and playing football in Florida.

"Every day that I wake up in south Florida—it's cold back home and there's snow on the ground and I don't have to shovel the driveway—it makes me feel like I'm getting paid to be on vacation for five years."

Award-winning actor Matthew McConaughey is a big Texas Longhorns fan. He was on the sideline when Texas beat Ohio State 24–21 to win the 2009 Fiesta Bowl.

Only once in the history of Connecticut football have the Huskies gone to a major bowl. That was the 2011 Fiesta Bowl, in which they lost to Oklahoma 48–20.

ASU went to half of the first 12 Fiesta Bowls, winning five times, including the first three. The Sun Devils have not gone back since beating Oklahoma in 1983.

GLOSSARY

All-America

Designation for players chosen as the best amateurs in the country in a particular sport.

campus

The grounds of a school, such as Arizona State University.

conference

A group of schools that joins together to create a league for their sports teams. The Big Ten Conference and Pacific-12 Conference are examples.

interception

When a defensive player catches a pass intended for an offensive player.

ranking

A national position as determined by voters.

sack

When the quarterback is tackled behind the line of scrimmage before he can pass the ball.

safety

A score of two points for the defensive team when the offense is unable to advance the ball out of its own end zone.

snap

The start of each play begins when the center hikes the ball between his legs to a player behind him, usually the quarterback.

two-point conversion

An option for teams that have scored a touchdown to try a running or passing play from the 3-yard line for two points, instead of kicking for one point.

underdog

The person or team that is not expected to win.

FOR MORE INFORMATION

Further Reading

Monnig, Alex. *Oklahoma Sooners*. Minneapolis, MN: Abdo Publishing, 2012.

Weinreb, Michael. *Season of Saturdays*. New York: Scribner, 2014.

Wilner, Barry. *Tennessee Volunteers*. Minneapolis, MN: Abdo Publishing, 2012.

Websites

To learn more about Bowl Games of College Football, visit **booklinks.abdopublishing.com**. These links are routinely monitored and updated to provide the most current information available.

Place to Visit

College Football Hall of Fame

250 Marietta Street NW

Atlanta, Georgia 30313

404-880-4800

www.cfbhall.com

This hall of fame and museum highlights the greatest players and moments in the history of college football. Relocated from South Bend, Indiana, in 2014, it includes multiple galleries, a theater, and an interactive area where fans can test their football skills.

INDEX

About the Author

Barry Wilner has written 49 books, including many for young readers. He is a sports writer for the Associated Press and has covered such events as the Super Bowl, Olympics, and World Cup. He lives in Garnerville, New York.